Patricia A. Smith

Patricia A. Smith

The You Behind The Eyes: Removing the Mask

Copyright © 2022 by Patricia A. Smith

ISBN# 978-1-7369051-0-4

Forward

Unmasking yourself is not easy but it's worth it. It frees you from all of the hurt and shame from your past. I was a beautiful Jewel stuck in a dark, low and lonely place. You don't have to be ashamed of what you've gone through in life, with healing and deliverance It can become a testimony. Throughout life people will assume this and that about you and sometimes even label you as things you've done or gone through but that's only through their eyes their perspective of you. When man said I was a diamond in the rough, God said You are my masterpiece. I've created you in my image and you are my chosen treasure. This book is dedicated to other women that have had their innocent, identity and safe place stolen by abuse, addiction and fear. You can find out who you really are when you develop an intimate relationship with God. He is our loving father and our safe place where we can come to him with the good, the ugly and the bad. I am removing my mask for you so you can remove yours for others. I want to thank the enemy for being my sparring partner during the training and development. I am grateful for the trials and the tribulation I've gone through in life. It helped mature my faith, wisdom and knowledge in my walk with God. NLT. Jeremiah 29:11 For I know the plans I have for you say, the Lord, they are plans for good and not for disaster, to give you a future and a hope. I would like for my sisters to continue this journey with me.

DEDICATION

I want to truly express how grateful I am to my family, friends and lovers for the life lessons and experience I've had throughout my life. I thank God for allowing each and every one of you to cross my path. I Am Forever Grateful

This book is dedicated to my mother Charlene Smith and my children Shi Smith, AnDarrius and Kayden Black. We've gone through so much together and I feel that telling my story is a chance for healing to begin in us as a family. In Jesus name I declare and decree that the generational curse stops here.

Special thanks to my grandmother, Shirley Smith, for always being there for me and my children. She is truly a blessing to her family. I want you all to know that I love you with everything in me.

I want to express how grateful I am to my family, lovers and friends for the life lessons and experience I've gone through. I want to thank God for allowing each and everyone of you to be a part of my life in the chapter we've

Patricia A. Smith

shared together. Today I live with no regrets and I am forever grateful.

ACKNOWLEDGEMENT

I want to thank my beautiful, intelligent, amazing childhood best friend Jamaeka Black for being there for me and editing my book with no hesitation when I asked. Thank you for sharing this experience with me, friend.

To MonTrelle Arnold I thank you for your patient wisdom and guidance in this process of publishing my book. I truly appreciate you for sharing your years of writing experience with me. He has made giving birth to this baby so safe and secure. Thank you!

With a sincere heart I want to thank Julian Neely for his encouraging words, for believing in me, keeping me motivated and for supporting me on this journey. Thank you so much!

Table of Contents

Safe Place

Let me introduce myself. I'm a country, Mississippi girl, born to an abused and very emotionally damaged 15-year-old. My father was a much older man that was in and out of my life during my adolescent years. At the time, we lived with my grandmother in this big, but very old house that had a pond out back. The house had cracks and holes. We didn't even have running water! We had to carry water jugs, and I remember heating up water to fill up the tub to take a bath. I was the first grandchild, so I was my grandmother's precious baby girl. She was this 4 ft 11 little woman, but she had a huge personality. My grandmother loved to go fishing and garden. She would take me out in the garden with her, but I didn't like getting dirty, I most definitely didn't like the bugs, and I didn't like fishing either. It seemed like she went fishing every single day. Just say I feared everything. I was with my grandma a lot, but while she was fishing; I would stay close to the house and play with my uncle. He was much older but mentally, he had the maturity level of a young child; so, it was still fun too. Have him around as a playmate. My uncle had this friend that lived across the street. He would come over to play with us. We didn't have much- or a lot of toys, so we found things in the yard to play with. They built a clubhouse from pieces of wood, tin and used old car seats for chairs. One day after school, they were waiting at the end of the driveway to get me off the bus. My grandmother was already gone fishing. We got there and started playing as always, but this time my uncle wasn't around as much. I found out that day that my uncle's friend was not interested in playing with him. He had his eyes on me the whole time just waiting for the opportunity to get me alone. He took me into the clubhouse and started touching me. I was only 5 years old, and I was scared and confused. My uncle showed back up, but he didn't catch him!

For some odd reason, I thought I would be in trouble if I said something. After that day he would be waiting for me to get off the bus. It happened several times! Over and over again, and eventually I would just close my eyes and pretend I wasn't there. That's when I learned how to become numb to certain things. The enemy had stolen my innocence and my safe place. After those incidents, I became quiet and shy.

There's a lot of things I don't remember after that. I think I blocked them from my mind.

My brother was born months later. At the age of 10, my mom got married and joined a COGIC church; so I went to live with her and my stepdad. It was just me and my brother for a little while, but she started having babies back-to-back. It felt like I had become the second mother and wife of the house. I had to do everything my mom did (as a woman of the house) besides sleep with her husband! Now I can understand chores, but it seems like I was in my own little ghetto Cinderella story. Those cloth diapers traumatized me because they didn't use Pampers and pull-ups back then. I would say to myself all the time, "I'm not having kids!" As times went by, I started feeling like my brother and I were outsiders. It seemed like we got in trouble for everything. Most of all, I hated when my brother got a whopping. I wanted to protect him, but I couldn't. I remember one day I was finishing up my chores for the night. I had cleaned the kitchen, bathroom, living room and mopped the whole house! My step dad walked in from work with the muddy boots and tracked up the floor. I said to him, "I just mopped the floor," and he said to me, "Well, that's why I got you here." Something went all over me, but I knew better than to respond. I was too tired to take a whooping that night. It seemed like my mom just wanted to keep the peace, so talking to her about it wasn't going to do any good at all. She was very loved by the other girls at our church and our neighborhood. She even took in one of them that wasn't that much older than me. They talked a lot, but we didn't click at all. I couldn't talk to my mom about anything. That hurt! It was church, school and home. We really didn't go anywhere or do much. The babies kept coming which made me very sad and depressed. I didn't get to do anything I wanted to do as a child, like play basketball, be a cheerleader, dance team or run track. I could barely play in our yard. I really shut down and didn't like to deal with people that much. I was so mentally drained, and school was just a getaway for me. My mind was so cluttered that I couldn't really think, function or learn like I needed to. That caused more problems because I was ashamed, afraid and embarrassed because I couldn't do my work and didn't have any help at home. My mom didn't finish school, so she couldn't help me. Church was another place to spend a lot of time, and I tried to make it a resting place. That didn't work because my mom was the usher, and she wouldn't let me fall asleep. She did not play about church! The only thing I liked about it was singing in the choir because I loved the music. We had different programs, and we would visit other churches often. That is how we got to meet other kids. There were too many rules! You can't do this! You can't do that! I couldn't do anything - anywhere! Talking about a prison…Sometimes I would go into my closet to cry. There were times when I begged God to not let me wake up. I thought about taking my own life, but God would meet me in that closet. It became my safe place. I would talk to God, not really understanding who he was, but I knew he existed. He gave me a little more strength to make it another day.

My Beauty Was A Curse

As the years passed, my mom had had five more girls! There was more hair to comb, more clothes to wash and iron, and more people to cook for. Now, I'm saying to myself, I don't want to be a wife or mother. Haha! Finally, she allowed me to start going to different places a little more. I went to my Dad's parents' house, my godparents, and my aunt's house. Excited to get away from all the crying, the pamper changing and the cleaning to find out there's still no safe place for me. It was like I was a target. Everywhere I went people were trying to molest me. One day, I built up the courage to tell an older cousin about it. I wanted her to be with me when I told an adult, and she said they're not going to believe you because I tried to tell them, and they didn't believe me. Back then, people had it bad sweeping things under the rug and would say, "What goes on in this house, stays in this house." I became bitter and angry because all I wanted to do was be a normal, happy child. I couldn't trust anyone! One summer I got to go swimming with a friend and her family. When I got home, there was no one there. I started changing my clothes so I could meet her at the basketball court. Her uncle walked in the house as I was about to walk out and push the door closed and raped me. It was like I froze! I couldn't believe that this was happening. The crazy part is after he finishes, he asks me if I have any STDs then rushes out the door! Again, the enemy had me in a corner. He whispered in my ear, "You can't say anything because you were smiling at him earlier. You made him do that to you." I was only 14! Now I'm saying to myself, just pretend it didn't happen. I did for a while, but I decided to tell a close friend which was later thrown back in my face when they got mad at me.

That hurt! I didn't have a connection or could talk to my mom about anything. I didn't like my stepdad because I thought he didn't like me and my brother. He would always whoop us for everything. I was starting to hate my dad because I felt like he should have been around to protect us. God where are you? Why is this happening to me? My shyness turned into madness, so I walked around with a frown on my face, trying to act mean and tough. I was called stuck up and other people said I thought I was more than everybody else. Haha! Can you say misunderstood? They just didn't know how much fear was behind the mask. Do you see why I thought my beauty was a curse? Now I'm going through life with extremely damaged emotions. Let's talk about some of those damaged emotions: 1) Fear: I had a great deal of fear and could never make up my own mind so I always found an excuse and usually never accomplished my goals. I suffered from low self-esteem and allowed myself to be controlled by others who promised to show me love and acceptance. I was easily manipulated and afraid to break away because of losing their attention and being lonely. 2) Super Sensitive: I have been hurt deeply and always needed love, approval and affection. That made me become a people-pleaser 3) Sense of Unworthiness: A continuous feeling of anxiety and inferiority. I thought I couldn't do anything right and that I wasn't smart enough. 4) Perfectionist Complex: Frequent fear of disapproval from others or feeling insecure and inadequate because I didn't think I could ever do anything well enough. Sounds bad huh? It was! With so much stress and depression from home, I moved back with my grandma. I didn't want to leave my brother, but I had to get away.

Fast Lane

Here I am 15 years old existing in resentment, bitterness and anger. Like most sexually abused children who begin to act out, I started living life too fast. My grandma was older and more laid back, so I started slowly slipping away. She would fuss and say something but not really enforce it, so I found some freedom. Freedom that I couldn't handle. I started hanging out with older friends and cousins. We would go to parties and clubs where they were drinking and smoking, so eventually I started drinking. Smoking wasn't really my thing. I was looking for acceptance and attention in all the wrong places. I knew that wasn't good, but it was fun at the time. I wasn't really excelling academically in school, so it was at the bottom of the to-do list. I was running the streets doing grown-up things, so I asked my aunt if she could talk to my mom for me. My aunt said I should, so again, I tried to talk to my mom to ask her about birth control. She said, "You don't need to be thinking about stuff like that!" Back then, everything was just-don't think about it, don't speak on it, and just don't do it. Now at the age of 16, I'm pregnant. Generational curses strike again. The molestation, being raped and now teenage pregnancy. WOW! The enemy is celebrating on my family's behalf. Two days before my 17th birthday, I gave birth to my beautiful daughter. I had so many different emotions going on, but thought to myself I could do this. I've had plenty of practice, and I had helped my mom with all of her kids! I also thought to myself, "My grandma will help me." I couldn't believe I was somebody's mother. Even though I felt I had been a mother pretty much all my life. This was a different feeling. I would just hold her and look at her. She was so little! For a while, I didn't want her out of my sight. My grandma would come into my room to get her and walk around the house with her like she was a football. She helped me a lot, so much, I had time to get back in the streets. Remember, I'm 17 now - so party, party, party! I'm back baby! My cousin and I were best friends. We hung out all the time. Even though I tried to go back to school, it was far from my mind and didn't last long. Eventually, I was so far behind I decided to get my GED. I took the test, but I wasn't good at using a timer. It gave me anxiety. I couldn't stop thinking about the clock. I passed it, except for one part. I scheduled a retest but didn't go back then. It was years later when I finally got my diploma from an online Christian school. As time went by, I started spending a lot of time with my boyfriend. We decided to move in together. I went to my grandma to talk to her about it, and she said, that's fine but you're not taking my baby, meaning my baby. I felt some type of way, but then I thought I was walking distance from where she lived so I could see her every day. It was best for her at the time because I was 19 and still too young- and living too fast. I was chasing freedom! My house became the hangout spot. I didn't know any better. I was so excited about having my own place and living with someone who loved and accepted me. We had a lot of fun at first, but with all of that drinking and partying the relationship became very toxic. Between all the profanity and breaking stuff every weekend, my first son was conceived. I got married at 21 and had the baby four months later. That slowed me down a lot, and reality set in. I had to grow up. I went to Cosmetology school because I had a gift for doing hair. I was the oldest of 6 girls, so I had a lot of practice, plus I did friends, family and church members' hair over the years. I loved doing hair, but I also made flower arrangements, sold Mary Kay and worked seasonal jobs at warehouses to build a good life for my family. The relationship was still very toxic, but I didn't want a failed marriage. Don't get me wrong, we had some fun times especially when we had gatherings. We started doing that all the time. It didn't matter what we were going through, I would forget about it because of so much laughter and love during the gatherings. I loved his family, and I know they loved me. One of his younger sisters became my best friend. We were extremely close, and we helped each other through a lot. An amazing, caring and funny family, but the reality would always set in. I was doing everything my mom taught me in her marriage, but I just didn't know that her marriage was toxic! I guess I wouldn't have known being a child and all. She finally got a divorce and moved on, but I didn't know how to let go. Those damaged emotions were also strongholds. The enemy had the deepest hook of fear rooted in my soul. Only God could free me from that demon. Depression found me again, this time it was harder because I had to try to function as well as I could for my children. One minute, I was fine and the next I was trying to drink myself to sleep. I was becoming angry, bitter and resentful in my marriage. It was like I had to grow up and be responsible, but he had his freedom. His mom and I would talk all the time, and she knew what I was going through. It was like she was my mother. She was the one that helped me to open up to my mom. Some time had passed, and my mom's house burned down so she came to live with me for a little while. She helped with the kids. My husband and I were growing farther apart, but I still couldn't leave. I decided to start doing what made me feel in control at the time, I started going out with my girlfriend. Really trying to show him I can do what he was doing. Seeking revenge isn't good. One night the kids went to my grandma, and my mom and her friend went out. I was home alone, just drinking, thinking and talking to God. I kept saying "Lord, I'm tired of this. This is not my life and I don't want to live like this anymore." I would say that to myself all the time. When I finally fell asleep, my phone started ringing and woke me up. My mom's car had broken down on the side of the road. I looked at the clock, it was 2:45am. I jumped up, got dressed and headed out. Remember, I had been drinking all night and was half asleep. I had a red 3000GT. I was driving fast on a very, very dark country road that I really wasn't familiar with. I came to a sharp curve going too fast to make it so my car started to flip about 4 to 6 times. It was like a movie. There were no streetlights, and it was black dark. I was terrified. There I was upside down in a ditch. I heard dogs barking. I was praying to God, "Please don't let me die like this." I never experienced anything so scary. When the car flipped, it flipped through someone's gate at the end of their driveway. They called the police, and coincidentally, they were down the street helping my mom get her car started. When the call came through, my mom told the police, "That's my daughter. She was on her way to get me." When they got there, they had to cut me out of the car. I had to be airlifted. I was hurting so badly. The hospital checked me out and found that I had four broken ribs, a fractured collarbone and a fractured pelvic bone. I had a stick stuck in the back of my head, something had cut into my ankle and glass was in my face. BUT GOD!! I knew then my life would never be the same. I had to change! I didn't want to die and leave my kids. When I got home from the hospital, I had to sleep on the chase because I couldn't lay flat due to the broken ribs, and I couldn't walk because of the fractured pelvis. As the days went by, I just slept, ate and took my medicine. My son would sit and watch me sleep. Every time I woke up, he was sitting right there. That meant a lot to me. My mom was a big help. She came through for me. I remember my sister-in-law and her friend coming over to pray for me. I really needed that. It took a while, but after I started back walking, I told God I would go back to church, and I did. That was also a scary process because of what I had seen growing up.

I just knew I would fail God because I couldn't keep all those rules. I tried, and I was doing pretty well but I was being taught religion. However, I was not developing a relationship with God, so my healing never really started. Living with anger, bitterness, rejection and many other strongholds, I fell again. This time I fell harder because I was confused and angry at God. I was like "I'm trying to do what you want, but you're not showing up for me." You're still allowing me to be hurt and abused. I wanted to know why I couldn't just be happy and free. At the time, I didn't realize God was allowing me to go

Patricia A. Smith

through this to build me and strengthen my faith in him, not to break me - but now I was becoming numb. I stopped caring about everything and everyone except for my kids, and I really couldn't care for them the way I should have. I left my husband, but it wasn't long before I went back. It was a very sensitive and emotional time for us. He had lost his mom, and she was like a mom to me. She was a very, very special lady that I will never forget. We would talk all the time because she had gone through similar things in her life. I remember her saying to me, "Baby girl, don't be like me." I miss her so much.

Shortly after that, I had another son. I know -I know! We tried for about a year to work on our marriage, but it didn't. At the age of 32, I left for good. I was tired, and it was nothing he or anybody else could say to make me change my mind. I was done with the marriage and even more damaged. I had to start over and alone. Now, I'm mad at him, God, and myself. My friend told me "Sis, just because you were married didn't mean you weren't doing it alone in the first place." She said, "You got this!" She didn't know about the deep-rooted hook of fear that the enemy had in me from the age of five. I knew I could provide for my kids, because I've always been a go-getter. It was my mental state that had me stuck. My grandma was always there for me and my children. I knew she would help me out as much as I needed her to. I tried to find myself, but with so much anger; I was drawing all negative attention. There were men that always wanted me, but I was married. I can still hear their approaches! "Baby, I know you are a good woman. You deserve a man that's going to spoil and take care of you." In my head, I'm thinking, that's all you can do for me because I'm not letting another person hurt me. Being numb to your emotions is a dangerous place to be. I was doing what I wanted to do, to whomever I wanted to do it to, and not really caring about anybody else's feelings. My love became very toxic. Now, I was the abuser. They say, "hurt people, hurt others." I was in a very dark and low place in my life. I didn't love them; I didn't even love myself. I did things I never thought I would do.Talking about the good, the ugly and the bad! No now, maybe in the next book. One day I ran into a friend of my friend, and I knew he was an angel. God used him to save me from myself at that time. I never had anybody to just talk to me. We could talk about anything. We just laughed and talked, and before you knew it, hours had passed. He helped me slow my life down, but he couldn't heal me though. The damaged little girl saw something different in this man and I didn't want to hurt him. I prayed to God that he would marry me because I wanted a new life and my family back. It had been 7 years since I left my husband. I really wanted to settle down. I knew he would be a great husband. That following year we decided to do it. I was so happy. We did everything together! We never argued. We would still sit and just talk for hours. I told him all about my childhood and everything I had gone through in my life. He did the same. We didn't have any secrets. He made me feel safe enough to let it all out. I've never felt safe with anybody. I had never had a best friend like him. You know the enemy didn't like that, so the marriage didn't last long. We had an incident happen, and the sacred little girl showed up. The fear that had never been dealt with or healed took over again. Misunderstanding the situation, I reacted out of anger and revenge because I thought he had done the same thing everybody else had done after I'd opened up and told him about the trauma. I believe God uses temporary assistance in the form of a human counselor who can help you perceive what the real problem is as well as incidents like this one. God wanted to heal me from my damaged emotions such as fear, rejection, anger, revenge and pride. I had to accept my responsibility in the matter. I asked myself if I wanted to be healed or do I want to use my problems to get sympathy from others. Some people become addicted to their problems, and it becomes their norm; but I wanted to be free in my mind, body, soul and Spirit -meaning willing to hear and accept the truth. God works differently with each individual. We must learn to follow God's personal plan for us no matter what our problem may be. God promised to meet our needs and repay us for our loss. Facing the truth is the key to unlocking prison doors that had me in bondage. I had to face my problems with honesty and with God's grace, I confronted the awful hidden memories within. Some problems can never be solved until you confess them.

NLT James 5:16. CONFESS YOUR SINS TO EACH OTHER AND PRAY FOR EACH OTHER SO THAT YOU MAY BE HEALED. THE EARNEST PRAYERS OF A RIGHTEOUS PERSON HAS A GREAT POWER

AND PRODUCES WONDERFUL RESULTS.

Some people miss deep healing because they don't have the courage to share deeply with another person. Many people are hurting and crying out for help, but they are not willing to receive the help they need from God. The truth is, no matter how much we may want help, we are never going to get complete healing until we are willing to do it God's way. Jesus said there's no healing taking place until there's deep forgiveness, so forgive yourself and forgive everyone who caused those problems. I never wanted to hurt him, but I know everything happened for a reason. If the incident never happened, I would have never dealt with my issues. I realized I really needed and wanted to be healed. I started seeing a psychiatrist and seeking God for myself. My psychiatrist asked me so many questions that I didn't have the answers to. I found out I didn't even know myself. She told me to start journaling my thoughts, my prayers and everything that came to mind. This is what I was doing anyway because that was how I expressed myself. One day, I was at work on my lunch break, and I saw a quote asking a man did he really know his woman. God said, "The question is for you." He said, "Do you know yourself?" God said, "They never knew you because you don't know yourself." Some of us have been wearing a mask for so long that when we meet someone, we introduce them to the mask. We don't know ourselves for several reasons. First ,we try to become what we saw Mama was as a woman, or we mimic other women, comparing ourselves to them. We become what people have told us as kids, what we've been taught, and we become who our spouse, friends and family wants us to be. Hello super you! The Super You is a false idealized image you think you must be in order to be accepted and loved.

Removing the Mask

As a Christian, you can be a realist. This means you don't need to be afraid to face the worst, the ugly and the most painful. Express your feelings of grief, sorrow, hurt, loneliness, struggles and even depression. There is a rugged honesty about the life of Jesus. Every kind of emotion was so clearly recorded and freely expressed without any sense of shame or guilt or imperfection. Take your pattern from Jesus not from some mythical super self. To be healed takes time through the power of the Holy Spirit and the application of God's word.

We must go through a certain amount of pain and discomfort to break out of mental and emotional addiction. Never be afraid to express your real feelings and your real self in Jesus Christ. When you waste time and energy trying to be super you, you rob yourself of growth and your relationship with God. God loves and accepts the real you, and this is the only you that he knows and sees. Super you is an illusion of your imagination, a false image and an idol. Jesus Christ has offered himself to redeem our soul. Now I know I don't have to settle for a life dictated by my insecurities or previous experiences.

God has given me access to the power that is working within me to free me from any mental and emotional bondage, but we cannot operate in that power and hang on to the excuse at the same time. Jesus gave us an opportunity for a fresh start, a new beginning. This means that anyone who belongs to Christ has become a new person and the old life is gone, a new life has begun. 2 Corinthians 5:17.

Letting the Healing Begin

After my second divorce, I told God that I wanted to live the life he created for me to live. An old friend from school came back into my life, and he took me to his church where I dedicated my life back to God and was baptized for the first time. I was 41 years old, and my soul had been lost for so long. I wanted a new life, and the only way was through Jesus Christ. If you knew me growing up, the outside was always fixed up with so much confidence, but my inside was fearful, insecure and crying out for help. My soul was screaming from the inside of a mental prison's wall, and the key was with God. Nobody knew the mental and spiritual battles I was dealing with. I was always fighting for everyone else, but nobody that I loved, cared for and prayed for, was fighting for me. In my weak moments, the flesh would get vulnerable. I would fall into sin that I thought I had moved past from, just to feel worse. It was like an emotional quicksand. Once I opened up the door to sin, the enemy's voice would speak louder telling me "You can never get it right. See, you messed up again, and God is not going to forgive you this time." When everybody else was asleep, I would lay in my bed and cry out to God, "Why can't I get this right?" I didn't want to do this. I really wanted to be free, delivered and live my life for God. It would hurt me so bad that I failed him again. Oh, but when you cry out to God with a sincere heart and as his child, there's something about the father's love that picks you up and gives you strength to keep fighting. God loves you as your father and doesn't condemn you. It's crazy! At those moments, sometimes I could hear my stepdad singing, "I just can't give up now. I've come too far from where I started from.

Patricia A. Smith

Nobody told me, that the road would be easy, and I don't believe he brought me this far to leave me."

Submitting to the Chase

I went through years running from the life I was living, but I should have been running into the arms of God. I knew I wanted something different, but I just didn't know where to start or how to make it happen. I remember I would change my whole house around every other month. The furniture, colors or whatever would make it feel new and different. I hated for things to be the same all the time. I would change my hair everyday or every other day, but that was only a temporary fix. The change had to come from the inside out.

Still shy and withdrawn from people, I continued to show up every Sunday for church because I knew I wanted to be free. I won't lie and say this journey was easy, but I was willing to fight through it. It wasn't just on Sundays when I would seek for God. I got up every day trying to find him. It was very lonely because I pulled away from everybody trying to find me. I felt so out of place as if I didn't fit in anywhere - anymore. I felt like my surroundings were suffocating me! I did hair for 20 plus years, but now I was starting to hate it. I thought to myself, "Did I even like being a hairstylist, or was it just a God-given talent that I couldn't avoid?" The only thing that kept me in that career was the smile I got after I was finished with my clients' hair. I always knew that I wanted to be a business owner with several businesses, but I let fear control me and hold me back. God put so many dreams and desires in my mind, but I didn't know how to execute his plan. During my healing journey, God revealed to me that I wasn't shy; but I was ashamed of what I had gone through. People labeled me as shy because I was so withdrawn. I took that title, stamped it on me and lived it out for years! See, the enemy knew who God created me to be before

I knew myself. That's why he wanted to keep me fearful and shameful. He had to do that to keep me quiet. He knew that God had chosen me, and that I would be a major mouthpiece and powerful woman of God. I asked God every day to allow me to see myself the way he sees me. I knew that there was more inside of me because of the desires in my heart. It was so much more than what I had seen growing up. I had encounters with a lot of different people saying the same thing. "Girl, there's something about you. You are something special. You are a very strong woman." Haha! I never could see it, but God had to reveal to me that some of the people that I knew had gone through similar things, and where they are in life. Some are on drugs, and some have lost their minds. I guess I was special and stronger than I thought by the grace of God. The enemy tried to use close people, places and things to distract me, but it was always something familiar. He knew how to get in my head. I made it a habit to wake up every morning and give thanks to God and submit my mind, my heart, my will and my emotions to him. I would pray to God. "I give you my mind so you can tell me what to think and tell me what to pray. I'll give you my heart so you can fill it with your love. God, please renew my mind and guard my heart." I thought, "That's a powerful prayer for anyone." My relationship with God grew stronger and stronger. He was teaching me how to love myself, and I realized self-love was very important. I read that self-love is the fuel that allows an individual to reach their fullest potential and is filled with compassion, grace and gentleness. Making space and prioritizing time for self allows us to embrace our lives completely and wholeheartedly. It's okay to put yourself first. It's ok to make space to identify your needs and wants because living behind the mask for so long clouds your ability to recognize what is absolutely essential. As women, we often find ourselves taking care of our children, our parents, our friends, and our lovers; but we often struggle to make space and time to put ourselves first. Maybe this came from my childhood wounds and deep-rooted trauma. Internalized beliefs of unworthiness are rooted in shame, and where the shame is self-love struggles to grow. I had to create a new foundation by setting healthy boundaries, new behavior patterns and beliefs. That was hard! People don't like it when you change even if the change is best for you.

Some people feel offended when you set boundaries. Some people can't handle your growth because they can only relate to who you used to be. Again, I say this journey gets lonely. It was ok though because I had to learn to be alone. I needed to spend time with myself to get to know myself better. I loved who I was becoming. I could sit in the house all day with no TV or anything on. Just me and God. I've never felt love like this. I think I was becoming addicted to God's presence. I think back to my childhood when I was sitting in my closet and this warm feeling would come over me. That was God the whole time. He really is my everything, so I knew I had to show up for him and his purpose for my life. It took me four years to start writing this book that God gave me so long ago. When I tell you fear "HAD" me. BUT GOD!! The enemy tried to tell me it was too late for me. I was too old, and I could never write a book. He was right. Not in my own strength, but God told me to expose my weakness so he could give me his strength. My God said I CAN DO all things through Christ Jesus who strengthens me. Philippians 4:13 Throughout my life, I journaled and would write things down all the time;

but because I didn't do well in school, I didn't think I was smart. God told me to stay close to him and that he was going to reveal so many things about me that it would shock me and even blow my mind. He is a father that cannot lie. I found out that I love nature. I love being near water, and I love to watch the sky. I realized I like being silly and making people laugh, so I had to think about it. I couldn't have been shy. I've even had the thought of being a Christian comedian. It's funny how I never knew who I was, but in my walk with God I had to die to the "me" that I'd become. God showed me the similarities in the relationship between my daughter and I and me and my mother. Growing up, I remember saying I would not allow my kids to hurt the way I did, but being a damaged child, trying to raise children was not good. I spoiled them and never wanted to discipline them because of what I had gone through. I wanted them to be able to talk to me and have the things I didn't have. I wanted them to be happy children. I didn't want to put them in a box. I just wanted them to live their own life. I gave them all the love I had to give but very little discipline. That wasn't being a good mother. As they got older, God revealed to me that my daughter was acting out my anger, my oldest son was living out the hurt I carried, and my baby boy was taking on the shyness spirit. That's why it is so important for healing to take place. I started speaking life into my children. They are who God created them to be! They are powerful men and a woman of God. They have a praying mother, and my God said everything attached to me wins. I know he is going to heal their hearts and renew their minds in the name of Jesus! I know now that God has chosen me to do great things, and this book is a part of my ministry and testimony. I have come a long way and I will do the good work that God has for me to do, but when a woman says yes to God; the enemy tries to intensify the heat. Those lustful spirits that were attached to me from childhood started showing up in my dreams. It knew it had no power when I was awake, so one night it came to me while I was sleeping. I know this is going to sound crazy to some people and some might not believe, but it's ok. This is going to help somebody. The spirit climbed on top of me and held my mouth so I couldn't say anything or move. I remember this happening before when I was younger, but I thought it was in my head. This happened throughout the year, but never to this extreme. I got a little scared, but I continued to try to fight it. It finally crawled off me and exited at the foot of my bed. I started crying and praying. I was so tired of dealing with this and being afraid. God said to me, "I have given you the power and the authority to conquer your enemies," so I continued to pray until I felt I was stronger. Ok, this time it was around 4 am. I got up to use the bathroom and got back in bed. I started going back to sleep and the spirit came back again. I couldn't move, I was trying to speak but my words wouldn't come out. I was trying to fight it with everything in me, but it raped me and left. Let me explain, for those in the natural mind, it was a wet dream I didn't want. I was so hurt and mad because I thought I was prepared for it. I cried and called out to God again. How can I fight it when I can't move or say anything? I'm tired of going through this. The devil spoke again, "It must be something you're doing. You're not saved! God is not with you!" Oh, I was so mad! I started praying and fasting about this battle. During this time, God said, "We are not fighting against flesh and blood enemies but against evil rulers and authorities of the unseen world, against mighty power in this dark world and against evil spirits in the heavenly places." EPHESIANS 6:12 He said, "Daughter, it was a spiritual fight." My God! The light came on above my head. In my dreams, I'm in the spiritual realm. Talking about spiritual warfare! It was months before he tried again. He was trying to catch me slipping because that's how the enemy works. He tries to be slick with his attack. This time I'm lying in bed watching YouTube and falling asleep. He came and snatched me to the side of the bed like he was trying to prove a point. I couldn't move, I couldn't speak!

I lay still and just started speaking in my heavenly language. I felt my body loosen up, and my mouth started moving. I sat up in the bed, and I declared and decreed that this was the last time. I told the devil he no longer has power over me, and I sent him back to the pits of hell with no return. I told him that God has given me the power and authority over him, and he must obey in the name of Jesus. That ugly spirit jumped up on the top of my bedroom door and looked back at me with so much evil in his eyes. I was face-to-face with the enemy. That was the last time he came to me that way. God told me, "You have to know who you are, who I've created you to be." In God, I am more than a conqueror. He wanted me to just keep showing up to the fight because it was already won. It's a fixed fight! He said, "The battle is not yours, but will you still show up to the fight? Do you trust God enough to show up for you?"

2 Chronicles 20:15 NLT He said, "Listen, all you people of Judah and Jerusalem! Listen, King Jehoshaphat! This is what the Lord says: Do not be afraid! Don't be discouraged by this mighty army, for the battle is not yours, but God's."

The Insecurity

It was so hard for me to move forward in ministry because I was insecure in so many ways. I didn't speak well for one. I took a speech class in school because I stuttered. I've always had problems expressing myself because of it. Whenever I was mad, excited, or nervous, my speech would become worse. I was also insecure about my appearance because I've struggled with my weight for a while. Having kids, drinking, partying, and my birth control also played a major part in my body's composition. All of it was a mental illusion to keep me from my purpose. The devil wanted to keep me quiet. He knows where you are mentally weak because it's what you believe and think about yourself. That's why it's so important for your mind to be renewed. The bible says to be transformed by the renewing of your mind. Ephesians 4:22-23 He would bully me every time I thought I was strong enough to go forth in my purpose. He knew who I was and what God had put in me before I even knew. Just to think, all this time, the devil was intimidated, insecure and afraid of me! That's exactly what a bully is! He knew the power that I carried, but

God had to reveal it to me. Have you heard the saying that a thief doesn't break into an empty vault? My vault had millions of God's children attached to my purpose. I remember spending time with God, and when he revealed how powerful I was; God brought back this article that I was reading one day about how this lady realized she had supernatural power when a car had fallen on her child. Think about the time when you thought your child or a loved one was in danger. Your courage and strength were beyond what you could have imagined, and you didn't have to think about how to react. When you operate in your supernatural strength, that is who you really are in the spirit. It has already happened in the spirit, but your natural life must catch up. The enemy knows that, and that's why he comes to steal, kill and destroy you before you realize it. But God!!

Forgiveness and Mercy

Boy I tell you, when you ask God to reveal yourself and what's hindering you from growing spiritually, be ready for it. This is how God talks to me. "Lil Girl". He calls me little girl when I'm responding from that broken child. He said, "Just forgive them!" Huh? "Yes!" But I thought I had forgiven everyone? Let me tell you how you'll know if there's unforgiveness in your heart. When that person says or does something, and it still affects you in a negative way, then you haven't let it go completely. He said, first forgive your mom because she was mentally and emotionally damaged. She loved and cared for you the best she could at the time. Forgive the abuser, my uncle's friend, that molested me at the age of five and the preacher man that raped you at 14. Oh yeah, I forgot to mention that he was a preacher earlier. I've thought from time to time that if I ever see this man, I would confront him to tell him he was wrong for what he did to me. God said, "Why? He knows he was wrong. Some people will never say I'm sorry, but you must forgive them for your freedom. They're going on with their lives, but you're stuck in bondage. Let me vindicate you. Forgive your father because he wasn't there to protect his little girl and robbed you on the security of knowing that you were his little girl." I do regret not having a better relationship with my dad and will never get the chance to tell him I just wanted to be daddy's little girl. I was so hurt! My daddy died in prison, and I hadn't seen him in years. Now I realize I must hold on to the few beautiful memories we did have. "Finally, forgive yourself!" Huh? "Yes!" But God I was an innocent child. "So was my son," he said. "You have been stuck in a victim mentality for years, but I sent my only son to carry the cross for you to be set free. Forgive and show mercy as I have." Like these young kids today, say nomo! Haha!

Come as My Child

God wants us to come to him as little children and have a child-like faith. Meaning believe everything he tells you is true and depend on him for everything. It's the same with you and your children. Think about it! When you tell a child something that's different from what their parents say, they will tell you, but my mom said this or my dad said that. They believe their parents. I've thought about the things we've told them that weren't true, like the Tooth Fairy. They have never seen a Tooth Fairy, but they believe there's one.

That's how God wants us to believe. We don't have to see it to believe, but we trust him enough to know that my father said it. This was kind of hard because I never had someone I could trust as a father in my life. God had to give me an image of me as a little girl with him holding my hand, swinging me around and dancing with me while I stood on his feet. You know like in the princess movies? I remember my mom telling me a story about my dad staying up all night killing mosquitoes so they wouldn't bite me. God said, "That's what I do, stay up all night watching and protecting you." There's another time when my dad didn't want me to talk to this guy. I didn't realize at the time he had heard and knew things about him that I didn't. God is the same way. He hears and knows what was said about you or what was not good for you. That's why he wouldn't allow certain people to come into your life or allow you to go to certain places. Protecting you from what you couldn't see or hear. God knows all and sees all.

Leap of Faith

I started a women's ministry in 2019. That was my first leap of faith, and I was so nervous. It was very scary for me because I had a fear of speaking in front of a lot of people. I was used to talking to women that came to my beauty shop, and it was comfortable because it was just us, but 31 women showed up to this meeting. I could have passed out! I've always had young ladies and family and friends that would talk to me about their relationship problems and other things they were going through. I knew it was something that

God had put in me to do, but I wanted to do it behind the scenes. I remember a dream I had about a woman giving birth. The lady was holding her baby close to her chest. She had strings attached to her body that flowed so far you couldn't see the end of them. God revealed that the baby was my ministry, and on the end of those strings attached to me were other young, hurting women. That's why I couldn't stay behind the scenes. There were women all over the world waiting for me to operate in my purpose. Their healing, breakthrough and their purpose was depending on me to come forth and speak God's truth. The second leap of faith was my YouTube channel. I was wondering how I would reach these women all over the world. God always has a plan, and our thoughts are not like his thoughts. I had to make up my mind to just do it, even being scared. God would say, "Lil Girl! In me you are strong". His strength is made perfect in our weakness. I was so nervous that I didn't even introduce myself. I started doing encouraging videos and sharing viewpoints that God was giving me. It wasn't getting any views, and I asked God, are you sure you want me to do this? Everybody and their Mama was already doing videos. I stopped because I really didn't want to do it anyway. It was almost 7 months later, God said go back to what I told you to do before. We were in this pandemic, so I knew he was talking about the women's meetings. Ok, let me just do this so I can go to the next thing. I posted another video and asked my friend to check it out for me. She said it was a beautiful testimony and very encouraging. I was like, ok God- let's do this! It still seems to be at a standstill, so I started a Facebook group. I'm getting more feedback on it. Finally, a leap of faith is this best seller book. I have to speak things into existence. I'm claiming it in Jesus' name. I will expect and accept the new life God has for! Let's see where (the next) chapter takes me.

Power & Authority

(Side note)

The first breath I take every morning, I give it back to God with thanksgiving and praise. That's how you get ahead before the enemy slips in. He's already planned his attack before you open your eyes. Whispering in our ear, this is going to be a bad day, oh my back is hurting, I am so stressed and so on. Not today, Satan! When we wake up, we need to come out swinging. Be intentional about operating in the power and authority that God has given us to conquer our day with victory. If we don't prepare, we will be speaking and agreeing with those lies the enemy has put in our minds. Now we have allowed him to set the mood for our day and walk around in a victim mentality instead of victory.

The Love Letter

Dear Lover and Friend,

I want to apologize for my toxic love. I didn't really understand at the time that I was selfish and damaged because I hadn't allowed myself to heal. I was giving you all of me, but I was broken and wearing a mask. I never meant to hurt you the way that I have. I believe that everything happens for a reason, and I believe we crossed paths because of life lessons. I don't regret any of it. You were what I needed in that chapter of my life, and I feel you needed me. I remember you saying that you've never had anyone like me before and that I was so different from the others. I was giving you the love that I was looking for, but no man could give that to me; only God could fill that hole in my heart. My heart was so damaged. I needed to be needed. Again, I apologize for my toxic love! I came into your life knowing deep down inside that I was never meant to be the puzzle piece that completes your life. I've left your life feeling convicted and disappointed in myself because I never wanted to hurt you. I really want to love you with everything in me, and I did. One day while spending time with God and thinking about the journey I had with you, he said to me forgive yourself. You've shown love that I've put inside of you, and now it's known that he can be loved past what he's experienced. Lover, now you know if I can be loved this way by the wrong one, imagine being loved by the right one. Look for that, beyond what you've experienced with me. Don't settle, because you deserve the best. I thank God for allowing you to come into my life. No love lost, lover and friend. I'm Forever Grateful!

Made in the USA
Columbia, SC
17 June 2024

36777975R00055